RONALD SEARLE

Searle's Cats

SOUVENIR PRESS

SEARLE'S CATS
first published 1967

This new and revised edition
first published in 1987
by Souvenir Press Ltd.,
43 Great Russell Street, London WC1B 3PA
and simultaneously in Canada.

Text and drawings copyright © 1967, 1981 & 1987 by Ronald Searle

Reprinted 1987, 1988

ISBN 0 285 62818 6

Printed in Great Britain by
Hazell Watson & Viney Limited
Member of BPCC plc
Aylesbury, Bucks, England

Inefficient cat captured by an astute goldfish

An exceptionally barren cat trying to hatch an infertile egg

Happy cat in its bath unaware that the house is on fire

A rather timid wolf in cat's clothing

Exhibitionist cat trying out certain effects

Two cats discover that love is a many-splendoured thing

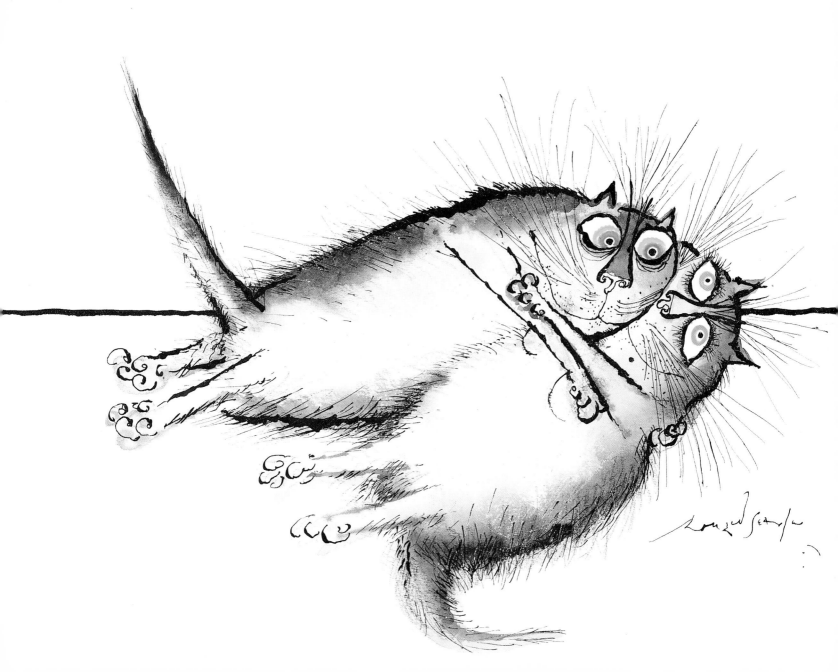

Embarrassed cat discovering that all cats are not the same in the dark

Cat of a thousand disguises concealing itself as a rug

A retarded cat trying to grasp a simple fact

Two cats quite calmly making beasts of themselves

Vegetarian cat regarding a plate of fried eggs

Exhausted Persian cat contemplating the advantages of monogamy

Unusually repulsive cat startled by a gesture of affection

Circus cat secretly rehearsing *Hamlet*

Gluttonous right-wing cat attempting to digest the left wing of a chicken

Remarkably hairy cat faced with the problem of dandruff

Cretinous laboratory cat under the impression that animals are exploring space

Acrobatic cat discovering quite unexpectedly that it is too old for the game

Balding cat walking out in an unsuitable wig

Young cat already regretting puberty